Light and Dark

Louise and Richard
Spilsbury

raintree

a Capstone company — publishers for children

Raintree is an imprint of Capstone Global Library Limited, a company incorporated in England and Wales having its registered office at 7 Pilgrim Street, London, EC4V 6LB – Registered company number: 6695582

www.raintree.co.uk
myorders@raintree.co.uk

Edited by Penny West
Designed by Rich Parker
Original illustrations © Capstone Global Library Ltd 2015
Illustrated by HL Studios
Picture research by Tracy Cummins
Production by Helen McCreath
Originated by Capstone Global Library Ltd
Printed and bound in China by CTPS

ISBN 978 1 406 29908 3
19 18 17 16 15
10 9 8 7 6 5 4 3 2 1

Spilsbury, Louise and Richard
Light and Dark (Exploring Light)

British Library Cataloguing in Publication Data
A full catalogue record for this book is available from the British Library.

Acknowledgements
We would like to thank the following for permission to reproduce photographs:
Capstone Press: HL Studios, 7, 18, Karon Dubke, 8, 9, 12, 13, 16, 17, 20, 21, 24, 25, 28, 29; iStockphoto: RapidEye, 10, SoumenNath, 11; Shutterstock: agsandrew, Design Element, Alexander Ishchenko, 6, ALMAGAMI, Design Element, Christopher Wood, 23, Click Bestsellers, Design Element, Dennis Tokarzewski, Design Element, EML, 5, GaudiLab, 22, ID1974, Design Element, Ivan_Sabo, 19, kurt, Cover, l i g h t p o e t, 27, luckypic, Design Element, Michelangelus, 14, Ryan M. Bolton, 26, Smit, 15, Vadim Petrakov, 4, Vass Zoltan, Design Element.

We would like to thank Catherine Jones for her invaluable help in the preparation of this book.

Every effort has been made to contact copyright holders of material reproduced in this book. Any omissions will be rectified in subsequent printings if notice is given to the publisher.

Contents

Some words are shown in bold, **like this**.
You can find out what they mean by looking
in the glossary.

Light and dark

Look around the room you are in. What can you see? Imagine you are looking at the same room when it is completely dark. What would you see then? The room would stay the same and everything would stay where it is – but you would not be able to see in the dark. You can only see the objects in the room when there is light. Darkness is what you get when there is no light.

We can see clearly in the light, but when it gets darker we cannot see things as well.

Light helps us to see in the dark and keeps us safe at night. The flashing lights on a fire engine warn us to get out of its way. Traffic lights tell drivers when to stop and go. The lights on a lighthouse keep ships from crashing into dangerous rocks along the shore.

Close your eyes.
This is what it is like in a really dark place. How would you find your way around in the dark if you did not have a light?

Lights help to keep us safe. Red lights tell drivers to stop at crossings. A green light in the shape of a person tells people when it is safe to cross.

Light and sight

We cannot see in the dark because we need light for sight. We see some objects because they give off their own light. Stars, light bulbs, candles and other things that give out light of their own are called **light sources**. We see light sources because the light they make comes directly to our eyes. Most of the things we see, such as books, balls, grass and people, are not light sources, so how can we see them?

We see some things, such as fires, when it is dark because they give off their own light.

We see most objects when light shines on them and bounces back to our eyes. When light bounces off something we say it is **reflected**. Light reflects off surfaces rather like a ball bounces off the ground. For example, other people can only see you when light bounces off your surface and reflects light to their eyes!

The Sun

The Sun is our most important source of light. During the day, its light reflects off objects all around us to light up our world.

When light from a torch bounces off a path and other surfaces around it, we see where we are going because some of that reflected light enters our eyes.

Activity: Make a dark box

How do we see in the dark?
Make a dark box to find out.

What you need

- a large box with a lid
- black paper
- sticky tape
- scissors
- a thin nail
- small objects such as a ball, a pencil and a coin
- a small torch.

What to do

1 Take off the lid and cut pieces of black paper to fit all over the inside of the box. Stick them on with the sticky tape. When you put the lid on, this will make a completely dark, black box.

2 Ask an adult to help you use the nail to make a small hole in one of the short ends of the box.

3 Put an object at the back of the box, opposite your peephole. Put the lid on the box.

4 Close one eye and look through the peephole with the other eye. Cup your hands around your eye to stop any light getting in the peephole. What do you see? Repeat for each of the objects.

5 Now turn on the torch and put it inside the box. Repeat steps 3 and 4 with each object. What do you see this time?

What happens?

When you look into the dark box without the torch, you shouldn't be able to see anything because it is completely dark inside. When you look into the dark box when the torch is on, you should be able to see all the objects because light **reflects** off them. We need light to travel to our eyes to be able to see. Light from the torch hits the objects and bounces back (is reflected) to your eye.

Brighter and dimmer

To read a book at night we turn on a bright lamp. In restaurants people often use candles to give a soft light. Some **light sources** are brighter than others because they release more **energy**. Energy is the power that makes things work or move. A candle flame has a small amount of energy so it only lights up a small area around itself. A big ceiling light that is powered by **electricity** releases enough light energy to light up a whole room.

A candle gives out a dim light that only lights the darkness immediately around itself.

Diwali is the festival of lights. Diwali candles would be barely visible in daylight but twinkle brightly in the dark.

Lights look brighter when they are closer to us. That is why it gets darker as you move away from a light source. Lights appear brightest when it is dark all around them. If you turn on a torch in daylight you will barely see its light, but at night torchlight seems very bright.

Star light, star bright

Have you ever wondered why some stars look brighter than others? A star's brightness depends on how far away it is from Earth and the amount of light energy it gives off.

Activity: Testing lights

Test how distance affects the brightness of an object.

What to do

1 Find a large room or space such as a hall that you can make dark. Make a chalk mark at one end to mark the starting point. Use the tape measure to measure two distances from this point, one at 3 metres (about 10 feet) and another at 9 metres (about 30 feet). Mark these distances with your chalk, too.

What you need

- chalk
- a tape measure
- two identical torches with new batteries
- two friends or helpers, including one adult.

2 Close any curtains and turn off the lights to make the room dark. Stand beside the starting point mark. Ask your helpers to take the torches and stand side by side next to the second chalk mark, 3 metres (about 10 feet) away. They should turn on their lights and shine them towards you. Look at the lights for just a moment. Compare the brightness of the two lights.

3 Ask one of the helpers to walk back to the third chalk mark, 9 metres (about 30 feet) away, shining the light towards you all the time. When they stop, compare the brightness of the lights again.

4 Now ask the second helper to do the same. How does the brightness of the lights compare now?

What happens?

When your helpers both stand 3 metres (about 10 feet) away from you, the lights look equally bright. When one moves further away, the closer light looks brighter. When they both move to the 9-metre (30-foot) marker, they both appear dimmer than they did from the 3-metre (10-foot) marker. One of the reasons a light could be brighter than another is that it is closer to us.

Day and night

Why is it light during the day and dark at night? The reason is that Earth is like a giant ball that **rotates** or spins. Every 24 hours it turns round completely. This means that when one half of Earth is facing the Sun, the other is turned away from it. The half facing the Sun is in the light, so has daytime. The half facing away from the Sun is in darkness and has night.

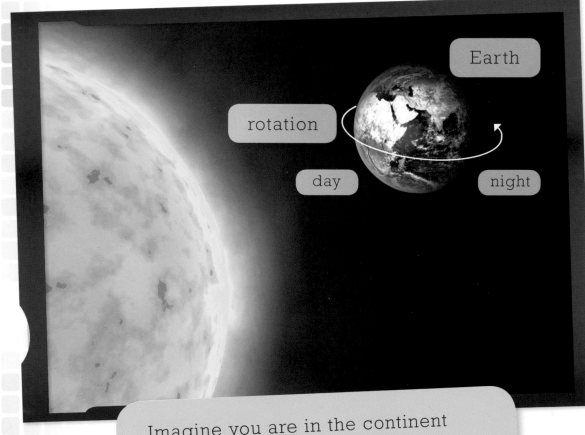

Earth

rotation

day

night

Imagine you are in the continent that is facing the Sun in this picture. What will happen there when Earth is facing the other way?

It is not always dark at night. Sometimes the Moon glows and gives off a soft light in the darkness. But the Moon is not a **light source**. Moonlight is just sunlight that **reflects** off the surface of the Moon!

Disappearing stars?

The stars are in the sky day and night. During the day the Sun makes the sky so bright that we cannot see the other, dimmer stars. At night, the Sun's rays are blocked by the other side of Earth, so we can see the faint light of the stars twinkling in space.

Activity: Making day and night

In this activity your head becomes planet Earth and experiences day and night, dark and light!

What to do

1 Ask an adult to help you remove the lampshade. Turn on the lamp. The light bulb that shines in all directions represents the Sun.

What you need

- a dark room
- a lamp with a lampshade.

2 Face the lamp and hold your hands either side of your face, with the palms facing forwards. Your head represents planet Earth. Imagine the North Pole is at the top of your head! Your hands mark the points east and west.

3 If your head were planet Earth, what time of day do you think it would be for a person located at your nose? Where would the Sun be in the sky?

4 Now, standing on the same spot, slowly turn a quarter way round to the right. What time of the day do you think it would be at your nose now? Turn a quarter way round again so your back is to the lamp. What time of day is it at your nose now? Turn another quarter. What is the time of day now?

What happens?

At first, when you faced the lamp (Sun) directly, your nose would have been in full, direct sunlight and if your head really were Earth, it would have been noon or midday around your nose. As you turned, your nose would have been at different times of the day: sunset, night, sunrise and then back to midday!

Colours of light

The sunlight that lights up our world during the day is called white light, but sunlight is not just one colour. It is made up of different colours mixed together. When sunlight **reflects** off different objects, some of its colours are reflected and some are **absorbed** (soaked up). This is how we see different colours.

When sunlight shines on a red apple, most of the colours are absorbed. The red part of the sunlight reflects off the apple, so we see the apple as red.

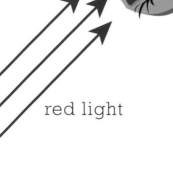

Sun

red light

sunlight includes all colours

We can see all of the different colours in sunlight when there is a rainbow. Rainbows usually happen after rain when the air is full of tiny water drops. As sunlight passes through the droplets, the different colours are separated so that you can see them. Have you ever seen anything else that can make a rainbow? You may have seen a crystal or an oily puddle reflecting light. The white light is split into the different colours. How many different colours are there?

A rainbow happens when sunlight is split into its different colours.

Activity: Make a rainbow

You can split white light into its colours to make a rainbow of your own!

What to do

1 Fill the shallow pan about halfway with water.

2 Lean the mirror at one end of the tray, at an **angle**. You might need some Blutac or modelling clay to hold it in place.

3 Ask a friend to use the torch to shine light at the part of the mirror that is under water.

4 Hold the white card above the mirror. Keep changing the angle at which it faces the mirror until you see a rainbow on the white card.

What happens?

When you shine the torch at the part of the mirror that is under water, the water splits the white light into all the different colours and a rainbow appears.

Dark and light surfaces

Which colour clothes do you usually wear on a hot, sunny day? Would you choose a light-coloured shirt or a dark one? Most people wear lighter-coloured clothing in summer because this helps them to stay cooler. Lighter-coloured surfaces **reflect** more light than darker ones. Dark-coloured surfaces **absorb** much more light and some of this light **energy** is released as warmth. When your shirt warms up, you get hotter, too!

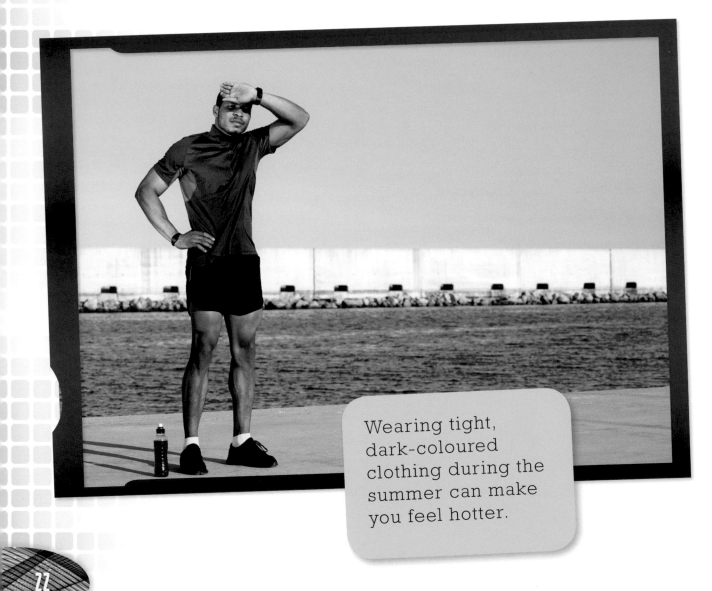

Wearing tight, dark-coloured clothing during the summer can make you feel hotter.

The white surfaces of the Arctic help to keep the area cold by reflecting away light energy that would turn to heat if absorbed.

Black and white colours are the best colours for keeping warm or keeping cool. A black surface is one that does not reflect any light. It is black because all of the colours of light are absorbed. As black absorbs the most energy, black surfaces also release most heat. White surfaces reflect all colours.

Arctic ice and snow

One of the reasons it is freezing cold at the Arctic is all the ice and snow there. These pure white surfaces reflect around 90 per cent of the sunlight that hits them back into the air. Ocean water only reflects 10 per cent.

Activity: Light and heat

Test whether the colour of a material affects how much heat it **absorbs**.

What to do

1 Wrap the black paper around one of the glasses using an elastic band or sticky tape to hold it on. Do the same with the white paper and the other glass.

What you need

- black paper
- white paper (the same type and size as the black paper)
- two identical drinking glasses or jars
- two elastic bands or sticky tape
- a measuring jug
- water
- a sunny day
- a thermometer.

2 Use the measuring jug to make sure you fill both glasses with exactly the same amount of water from a cold tap. Leave the glasses outside in the sunshine in a safe place such as on a table.

3 After a couple of hours use the thermometer to measure the temperature of the water in each glass. What do you notice?

What happens?

Dark surfaces, such as the black paper, absorb more light than lighter ones, such as white paper. The light that is absorbed turns to heat. You should find that the temperature of the water in the glass with the black paper around it is hotter than the one with white paper around it. This is because lighter surfaces **reflect** more light and so stay cooler.

Animals in the dark

We need light to find our way in the dark, but some animals have eyes that allow them to see at night. Many **nocturnal** animals have large eyes to collect more light. This helps them see in dim light. An owl's eyes fill over one half of its head and each one of a tarsier's eyes is the same size and weight as its brain!

The tarsier has the biggest eyes of any **mammal** compared to its head size.

A hare's large ears are constantly twitching to help detect and hear small sounds.

Some nocturnal animals use hearing and other senses to find things when it is too dark to see. Cats have ears that turn and twist to help them hear exactly where a sound is coming from. Rabbits and hares have long ears to help them hear foxes and other animals that try to eat them. Some nocturnal animals have a strong sense of smell. A fox's large ears hear well and its long nose helps it to sniff out **prey**.

Cats' eyes

At the back of a cat's eye there is a special layer that **reflects** light and doubles the amount of light they can use. When you see a cat's eyes glowing at night, you are really seeing the reflected light.

Activity: Super senses

Try this test to find out how our sense of hearing can help us "see" in the dark.

What to do

1 Sit your friend on a chair with the blindfold on.

What you need

- a friend
- a chair
- a blindfold
- a selection of items that make noise, such as coins, a book, a newspaper, a ball, paper, aluminium foil, a stapler, a bottle of fizzy drink
- a pen and paper.

2 Stand about a metre (3 feet) away and make noises with your different items. Bounce the ball, crumple the foil, undo the bottle of fizzy drink, close the stapler. Can your friend guess what is making each noise? Write down their answers.

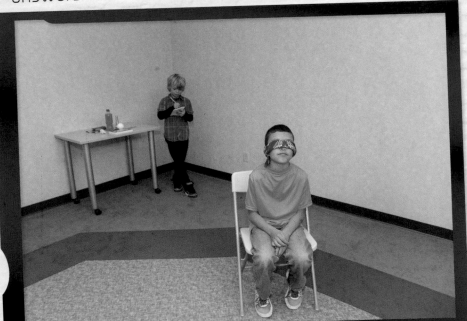

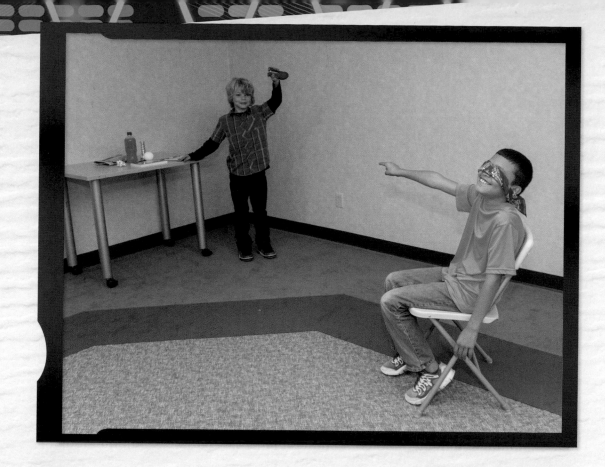

3 Ask your friend to cover their ears while you move to a different spot further away. Make a noise again. Can they point to exactly where you are standing? Move again and ask them to point to where you are again.

What happens?

Your friend probably got a lot of answers right. When our eyes are closed and we concentrate, we can use our sense of hearing to tell us a lot about what is around us.

You should also find that the blindfolded person can point to where you are quite accurately when you make a noise. Our two ears help us judge direction and distance. The ear closest to the sound hears it a little louder and slightly sooner than the other ear.

Glossary

absorb to soak up or take in something

angle amount or measure of a turn between two straight lines that meet at one end

electricity type of energy we usually use to make machines work

energy the power that makes things work or move

light source something that makes or gives off light, such as the Sun or a torch

mammal animal that usually has some hair on its body and gives birth to live young that feeds on milk from its mother's body

nocturnal to be active at night

prey animal that is hunted and eaten by another animal

reflect to bounce back light off a surface

rotate to turn in circles around a central point. Car wheels, merry-go-rounds and spinning tops all rotate.

Find out more

Books

Glaring Light and Other Eye-burning Rays (Disgusting and Dreadful Science), Anna Claybourne (Franklin Watts, 2013)

Light (Amazing Science), Sally Hewitt (Wayland, 2014)

Light and Colour (Straight Forward with Science), Peter Riley (Franklin Watts, 2015)

Light and Dark (Light All Around Us), Daniel Nunn (Raintree, 2012)

Websites

www.bbc.co.uk/learningzone/clips/day-and-night-on-earth/1874.html
On this BBC website the animation shows you how we get night and day on Earth.

www.bbc.co.uk/schools/scienceclips/ages/5_6/light_dark.shtml
You can investigate light and dark on this BBC website.

www.childrensuniversity.manchester.ac.uk/interactives/science/earthandbeyond/shadows
Find out more about how day and night happen on this University of Manchester website.

www.glasgowsciencecentre.org/online/dark-and-light-day-and-night.html
Join Jack and Alice as they explore the concepts of dark and light in an animated story on the Glasgow Science Centre website.

Index